Ruby at the Gate

Story by Robert Moses

Illustrations by Erika Cummings

Dedication:
To Casi, who started it all and to Smiley who made it fun.
We miss you dear friends.

1 3   5   7   9   10   8   6   4   2

Library of Congress Control Number: 2018952534
Ruby at the Gate
by Robert Moses
illustrated by Erika Cummings

p. cm.
1. Juvenile Nonfiction: Animals—Baby Animals—Lambs
2. Juvenile Nonfiction: Animals—Farm Animals

I. Moses, Robert, 1943– II. Cummings, Erika, 1994– III. Title.
ISBN 13: 978-0-9992885-3-5 (softcover : alk. paper)
ISBN 13: 978-0-9992885-4-2 (ebook)

Mariner Publishing
A division of Mariner Media, Inc.
131 West 21st St.
Buena Vista, VA 24416
Tel: 540-264-0021
www.marinermedia.com

Printed in the United States of America

This book is printed on acid-free paper meeting the requirements of the American Standard for Permanence of Paper for Printed Library Materials.

Introduction

In the spring, a ewe gave birth to the first of three lambs. It was a female and very frail. The mother tried to get the lamb to stand and feed, but it was too weak to move. The second and third lambs were about to be born, so the mother left the little lamb by herself. The Shepherd, who was in charge of the flock, took the lamb inside the farmhouse and gave her some milk. She ate very little at first and then ate more and more as the days and weeks went by.

Soon she was strong enough to live in the barn and join the rest of the sheep in the barnyard. The little lamb had no one to watch over her and keep her safe while she played with the others, so the Shepherd put a red mark on her back so that he could tell her apart from the other sheep as he watched her from a distance. The Shepherd would walk to the barn and feed her with a baby bottle four times a day. Needless to say, the lamb, whose name was "Ruby," looked forward to each and every visit.

The following is a story about that little lamb and her Shepherd.

A sound can be heard—it's my morning date.

It's feeding time,
and Ruby is at the gate.

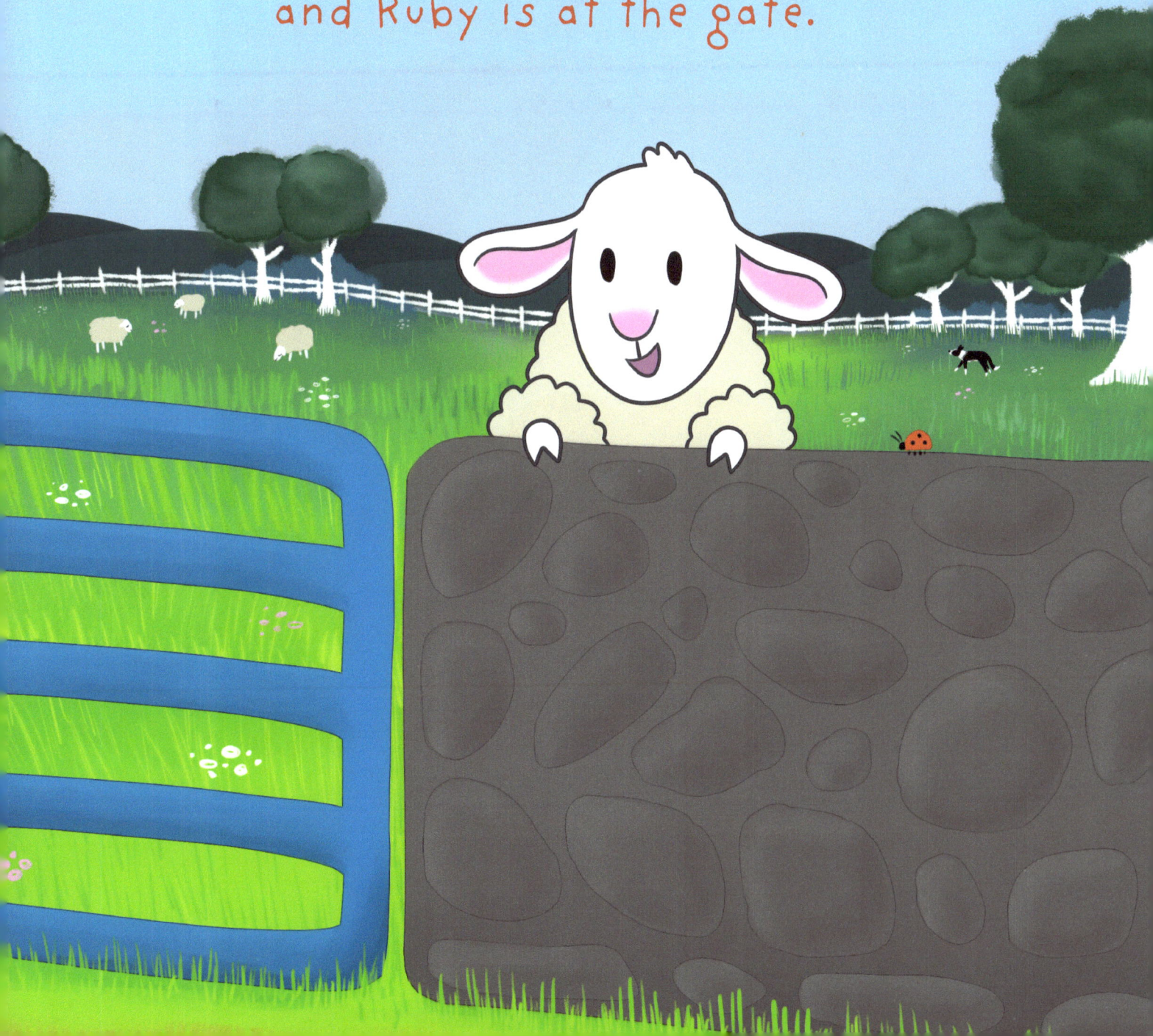

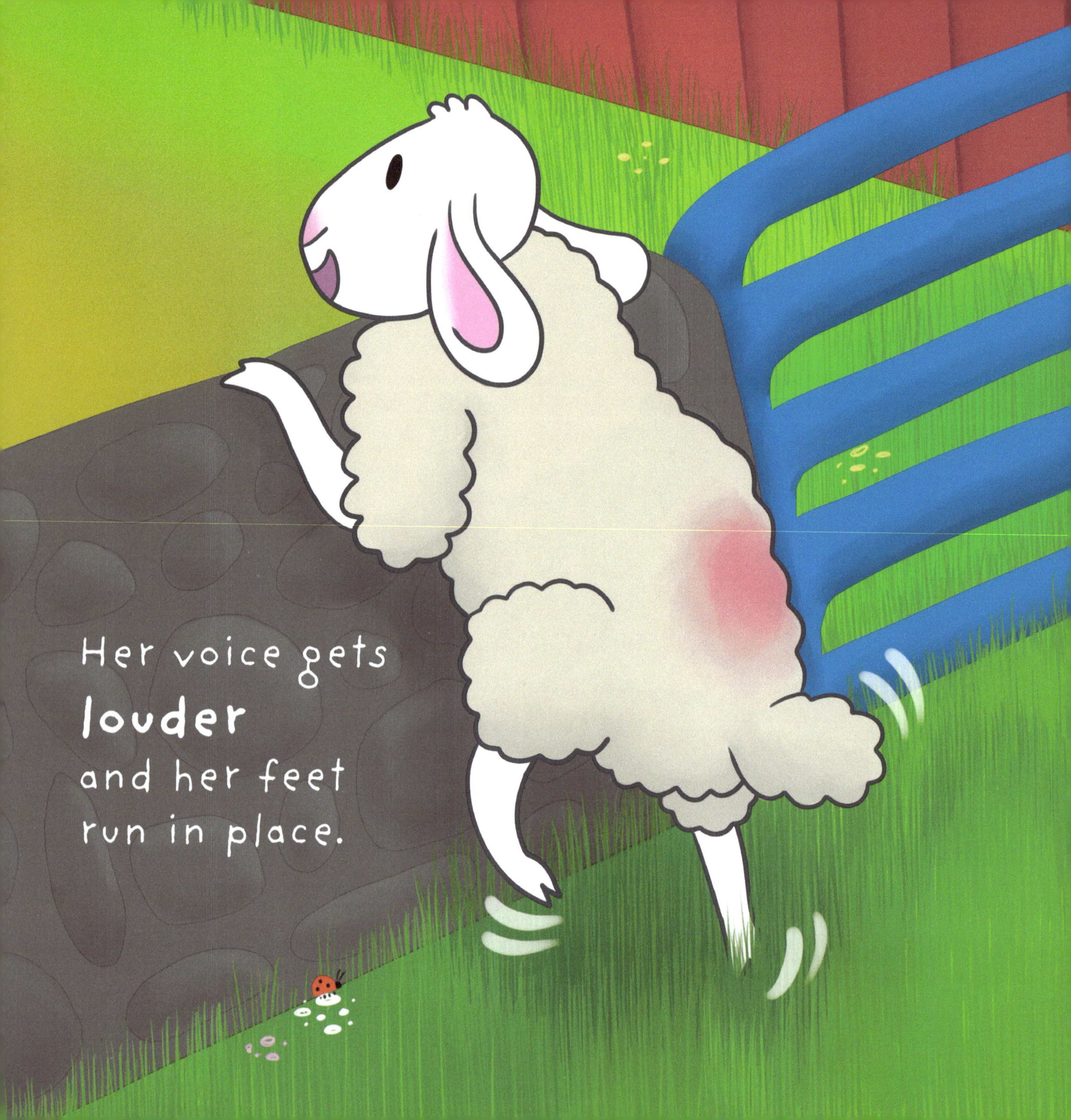

Her voice gets
louder
and her feet
run in place.

The others make way
and give her some space.
For each is aware
that they must wait,

When it's feeding time
and Ruby is at the gate.

I quicken my pace—
it's not good to be late.

At last I'm here,
and Ruby is at the gate.

I lift the latch to soften her mood.

She blows right by me,

and heads for her food.

And when she's done, no thanks do I get.

Down the hill she goes, for now she is set.

And even when she's grown and gets a mate,

It will be me
that she calls to when

Ruby is at the gate.

The End

Ruby and her friends live on a farm in the Shenandoah Valley of Virginia.

Although she is in the pasture with the other sheep, Ruby still comes running whenever she hears the Shepherd's voice.

She knows she will get some extra grain or a handful of alfalfa hay or just a scratch under her chin. (She really likes that!)

www.ingramcontent.com/pod-product-compliance
Lightning Source LLC
Chambersburg PA
CBHW041224040426
42443CB00002B/84